Real Monsters

Written and photographed
by Nic Bishop

Collins

What is it?
What is peeking out from the moss?
Is it a monster?

It is a lizard.

It is out and about, looking around.

It looks here and there.

But what is it looking for?

Plip! Plop!
The lizard plods across the moss.
It sees a frog on a leaf.

4

The lizard is not looking for a frog.
It plods away and creeps onto a branch.

Wait!
The lizard sees something on the branch.

It is a snake.

The snake spots the lizard.

It leans across and looks hard.

The lizard stops.
It stays as still
as a stick.
It looks like
a dry leaf.

8

The snake slinks away. The lizard is safe.
It plods on along the branch. It looks
this way and that way and all around.

Stop! What is that?
The lizard spots something
jumping in the grass.

It is an insect.

Zip!

The lizard acts fast.

It zaps the insect and sucks it up.

Munch! Crunch! Chew!
That is the end of the insect.
The lizard has found its lunch.

Real Monsters

a lizard

a frog

a snake

an insect

Ideas for reading

Learning objectives: Blend phonemes for reading; Read high frequency words on sight; Use phonological knowledge to work out and check the meanings of unfamiliar words and to make sense of what they read.

Curriculum links: Science: Variation – grouping animals and plants.

Focus phonemes: ea (real, lean), ew (chew) a-e (snake, safe), ay (way, away)

Fast words: what, the, here, there, onto, like, all, something

Word count: 187

Getting started

- Write the words that feature the focus phonemes *ew, a-e, ay* and *ea* on a small whiteboard and ask the children to fast-read them, blending aloud if they need to.

- Practise reading the irregular high frequency fast words by sight, in preparation for reading them in the book.

- Before looking at the book, discuss: *What is a monster?*

- Cover up the photo on the front cover and read the title of the book together, blending along the words Ask: *What do you think a **real** monster could be?* Reveal the picture.

Reading and responding

- Give out copies of the book for children to read independently.

- As you listen in, encourage the children to use an expressive voice for questions on pp2–3. Ask the children to answer these questions themselves first, then refer to the text. Can they predict the answer to the question on p3?

- When children have finished reading, use pp14–15 to talk about the different animals and what you find out about them in the text.